THUNDERBIRD

JANE MILLER THUNDERBIRD

COPPER CANYON PRESS

PORT TOWNSEND, WASHINGTON

Copper Canyon Press is in residence at Fort Worden State Park in Port Townsend, Washington, under the auspices of Centrum. Centrum is a gathering place for artists and creative thinkers from around the world, students of all ages and backgrounds, and audiences seeking extraordinary cultural enrichment.

LIBRARY OF CONGRESS CATALOGING-IN-PUBLICATION DATA

Miller, Jane, 1949–
 Thunderbird / Jane Miller.
   pages cm
 ISBN 978-1-55659-441-0 (pbk. : alk. paper)
 I. Title.
 PS3563.I4116T48 2013
 811'.54—dc23

                      2013003271

              987654321 FIRST PRINTING

COPPER CANYON PRESS

Post Office Box 271

Port Townsend, Washington 98368

www.coppercanyonpress.org

ACKNOWLEDGMENTS

Grateful acknowledgment is made to the following print journals and literary websites in which these poems, some in different form, first appeared:

Back Room Live, Boston Review, Boulevard, Lana Turner, Matter Journal, Poets.org (Academy of American Poets Poem-A-Day), *Sonora Review, Spiral Orb, Timber Journal.*

"Purple Field" and "& Darkness Moves In" each originally appeared in *Narrative* online as Poem of the Week.

It is not for us to greet each other or bid farewell is from "Elegy of Fortinbras," *Selected Poems of Zbigniew Herbert,* translated from the Polish by Czesław Miłosz and Peter Dale Scott (Ecco Press, 1986).

for Valyntina

Contents

THUNDERBIRD

ECSTASY

As the ancients detail it
ecstasy passes over us
in a mist of particles
it lives bare
dies unburied
I finally understand it is raining
it is beautiful
a couple of hawks in a tree
and not the tree entire

THE TREE ENTIRE

My brain lies crushed sideways
in a pillow of a morning

I hear you both faintly
deciding whose fields to empty

to clear-cut first growth
knowing such an odious decision

is prompted by a greater emergency
a fire on your watch

where officially a firewall is called for
I accept your predicament

your view obstructed
from your dark red couch

on a nearby planet
as two shining stones

you think the friction between you
is blazing hot and not just

death's genitals
which are a part of nature

NATURE

Do we need time to vanish
and to reappear like childhood
religious music?
it's stirring isn't it?
but *not for us*
as Fortinbras says to Hamlet when he's dead
to greet each other or bid farewell

where spooked horses refuse chase
we have only brute memory
without a wishing well
we are like gypsies with pink mandolins

against oblivion
we are gypsies with yellow wrist bells
a melting piccolo and a melting piano

WISHING WELL

The next day nearly kills me
along a frozen river or so I hear

the chaos around an old house
intimidating purposefully

like a snowplow one would assume
but it would be your human sound

scraping the white space from this page
has awakened me

now that you understand power in private life

you see my sore loser's blanket over my head
stemming a slow internal bleed before you leave

like a cat loose among hounds
that I do not think got killed by accident

ACCIDENT

During the ritual of dishes
I cut my trigger finger
breaking last night's crystal

needing stitches
like I dreamt I would
as an intruder stomping the glass

at a Jewish wedding
between the living and the dead
as between one day and another

darkness crashes down
Goebbels in disgrace over an affair
with a Czech actress deigns to instruct

police not to interfere
with rioters smashing windows
of shops and synagogues

Goebbels the beetle grub eats voraciously
before climbing into his armored car
the bark beetle scrapes the inside of a pine

until the whole forest is ravaged
I have no right to claim
our peoples' nightmare

familiarity with victims
hiding in villages along the frontier
but I beg that

if so much as one person
is made to feel shame with a mark
passed off as innocent as lipstick

smeared on a tumbler in a bar
it is in fact a branding
incapable of being

expunged even in ignorance
one must know the difference
because if so much as one

is shattered by a remark
hurled like a rock through a window
all of us have blood on our hands

& DARKNESS MOVES IN

I am bleeding through
the emergency
of my old body

no don't make the trip down
some pleasant resident
is sewing my finger back onto a stranger

STRANGER

It's a dog's life isn't it?
the dead cowards our guides
on a tear through the beleaguered fields
I could have said *tear* but if I am a powerful figure
an empire
I am not going to cry anymore

EMPIRE

Is nothing running through the fresh mustard fields
in our heads? is that why we leave for a cold place
a moon-walled grief

that turning in bed scares off? the dead—
I don't understand what they are fleeing—

(I could have said *what they are feeling*)

FEELING

I miss a shot at a fleeting figure
because I'm hunting butterfly
loaded for bear

LOADED FOR BEAR

This gun is a metaphor
whose drunken
shots one can still see through
the wooden family door to infinity

love rides
the high-speed bullet
like a fury

and you know
it fits into the story of my sad pony—

MY SAD PONY

It's a bougainvillea-ed viny
Southern California hotel
and next door my dead father is singing
in the shower I swear
hotel life is as demanding
as killing something sick
ever is

self-respect that is hard-fought for
and principles too are really lost
whereas a soul safely dead
is temporary

—freedom
travel and poetry
my beloveds
are finally gently provisional
a trust that is all feeling
without thinking
ecstasy—

WITHOUT THINKING

Is it history
that surprises you
publicly by whispering
and smelling your brushed hair?

perhaps we fully dress
in front of a fire before we alight
in any case you both look dazzling
in your encore—is the cure

stopping and setting the date
you would be fixed in the past
performances you loved most?
you select wartime

with your husband clerking and before your abortion
eventually another child and suburbia are admitted
like strange bedfellows one pays for the other
that's how I understand terror is

acquired—

ACQUISITION

Please let me not lose an hour
to rhapsodize a moment
let me take this flagrantly
engorged city

you have left me
as a compliment and a gift
I understand loyalty

LOYALTY

Without leading with your shroud
exposed to clouds and sky
you recognize me now with women
laughing very loudly on my arm
on medications whatever etc.

DOMINION

How's your writing going?
(Ought I to bring a gun on this trip?)
You write beautifully

CAMEO

What do you want to happen next?
I hope sincerely it follows
I am the world's worst compass
just curious
getting lost with your son looking
for the stone wall between
your graves and god's will
now that you are closer to rejection than to us
if there is no wall please
shall we thank god or the hilly ground
for a view of your inscriptions?
—the carved surfaces that lead us to wonder

LEAD US TO WONDER

Let's presume your savior exists before whom
you wished us to place your monuments
in the loam of Long Island

why is someone from time immemorial
hiding young consenting adults
in the dark must of a cemetery

for a release of warm semen
in order to disturb you
sentient unconditional beings?

because the darkness transforms them
from ninety seconds of space
into cypresses & stars

the implication being that evening
may not be a soft kiss in a kitchen
but a storm strobed with coyote

where lovers hide in pools of light
despite god knowing
that the choice is safe passage

or fair warning granted
I know I really can't call out anymore
I have forsaken your bloody hounds

BLOODY HOUNDS

A lion idles and a snake uncoils
under the spell of a full moon

their mortal wounds are invisible for the time being
resting in the shadow of the Almighty

torn and purpled and tired
my poor people await instructions

to tread upon the lion and the cobra
to trample the young lion and serpent underfoot

intent upon that inconsolable alarm
their sorry nervous systems get the better of them

they jump up as if elves
sourced a bell deep in their dreams

but for a moment of eternity
they no longer hear such sweet music

BELLING THE LEADER OF A FLOCK OF SHEEP

Celan and Mandelstam depart in a boxcar
before strangely burning down to darkness

each Jew is cold and unspoiled
a stone potato

that thugs fork and brandish
but whosoever pulls this sword from this stone

shall be the rightful heir
whereupon free spirits everywhere withdraw

jewel-handled blades from history's ribcage
and in no time the living inhabit the beautiful

loam and moonlight of an old world
of ripe figs and pickled herring

against unprecedented evil
the act of writing of apples

shoe polish and steaming potatoes
for history is heroic

at best an ordinary impossible struggle
pitting the living

against death the old country
where horseradish grows tall along a fence

METAPHOR

When one cannot otherwise
reverse a malignancy

or rewrite a child or an adult shot outright
suicidal or starved one by one
each questions authority or else the seed word

author lords over us all
one might presume *painlessly*
as it is only language

and this would be our first
mistake together

TOGETHER

However pale the pearl
light from above
just as insanity arrives uncandled
the missing
feel not one emotion
love desire fear and so on
without thinking of wars and worse
enforced laws against so-and-so for such-and-such

SO-AND-SO

I see myself clearly
who's sick here

poured into tight pants
and later undressed save that
I'm stranded in a necklace

of closing time
drinking chaperoned
by the cosmos

one dog day and night arguing
that spirit as much as any body
is severely limited

in its emotion
the will is not free
is what a friend said

after my breakdown
but gets it up faster than a porn star

STAR

Neither money nor honey much
matters only breathing so my shame
clamping down my lungs with its fuselage

is not helping it's not fitting
that some die while I go free

some nobody decides *shun shun shun*
and it has a sound with a shape
of freakazoidal afternoon shadows

FREAKS

Caused by bombers breaking another barrier
these pocks punched in blue sky
by evening become a monstrosity with *a shithole*

as my father used to say *for a mouth*
and this is how I imagine the murdered feel kissed
by their perpetrators at the ferry when they dock

to be escorted to dinner and ordered an obscure California vintage
they are damaged and able to speak only in tongues
of how the furies treated people

among whom I have a passing resemblance

RESEMBLANCE

We were driving
debating twilight
and what evening meant about dusk

we hoped to learn the instant
night falls and too late
although we saw the first star
said *not yet*
then Venus *not yet*
moonlight *now? no*

this is how I fail again
to let you go
I never hear the orders

finally in your twin beds
in your shells you say
Janie we love you anyway

I bury one in the sun immediately
and the other in the rain soon after

then another night
with the bar closed and the bed covered in clothing
a rat kills a chipmunk
a dog snaps the neck of a cat
a dog mauls a smaller dog
a gunshot kills a deer

the dead deer dying is now dead
sorry I have to let you down so sorry
your personal moon is blown away
by the ultra-gun of tomorrow

FUTURE

Beyond this happiness of mind-numbing
bloodied noses and buckteeth marks
there is a neutrality
about you now
I sense you are pulling yourselves out
of some fear-fuck
something forbidden
or softer in German
verboten—

VERBOTEN

My darklings can you protect my lover and me
from a nightmare of fish
being sliced with a sharp and sacred knife
and served as raw flesh
on porcelain cured at very high heat?
as human skin procured in the ovens of far cities
served God

FAR CITIES

I am powerless
and ask for your sword
I ask forgiveness

FORGIVENESS GRANTED

Fred rushes Stuttgart's airport
like a pilot a day late for his plane
what does he do in Germany?
his luggage is a gold ring
the day is fine it is the night

rumored to be cool and foggy
that has me edgy
we travel several bridges together
to select your casket unfortunately
brought low by resinous perfume

your son faints among the evergreens

EVERGREEN

A fir denuded of its flat leaves
rests on its side smelling

of the black salt seas as my brother my bellwether
slowly revives he hears you

our orphaned father scratching
in the wood box in the parlor like a rat

in steerage you grunt
uncomfortably from that old country

now is not a good time
but I never turn back

never guess that you're still here
in the ionized air of the white pine

in your right mind for the wrong reason
eternity

TIME

looks like someone sleeping
more than I am used to

a violet crocus closed
as patient
as spring is of snow

SNOW

She steers her children relentlessly
along autumnal palisades
in a fleeting two-door
across a steel suspension bridge

from the suburbs to a game at the Garden
she takes the turns tightly on surprise snow
in a superb red Thunderbird
her son daydreams he's a regal athlete

her daughter already is an accomplished servant
having escaped through the family room to rendezvous
with an art student under a weeping willow
both so young now long dead

NOW

Their familiar is newly licensed to drive around
their sartorial lives as sportsman and slut
silver braces set her brother's teeth
but the girl refuses intervention
she assumes the role of the intruder

their parent is a part of history and its provincial theater
with her sister Rachel—each with a first kid
abandoned to their mother Goldie
would steal afternoons at the movies
to dream of leading men

LEADING MEN

It is years before they are delivered
of second children cars single-family homes
and husbands unleashed from war
not yet human enough
I confuse desires for assignations
in the ignoble role of her admirer
I compete for mother's projection
on a blank screen I am born
and no sooner am back home
with mother and father buried
my brother and I light tapered
candles to see them more clearly
at the oval dining table holding hands

with mother I allow
she could crush mine
as she warned
if I lose my mind
she will have the advantage physically

PHYSICALITY

Dead you both stare down
candle after candle
into a quiver of moonlight

not a soul believes my sob story
in something this tight and exquisite

EXQUISITE

Did I say *hearts?* I mean to
rake yours outside when I weed

but I'm in here writing
moving one hand one inch
I touch the sheets to uncover you

DEAD

Our childhood such a large cellar with no bulb

LIGHTS

As night falls toward your mysterious bodies
the smaller it gets it glows
darker in my head
until clearly my loves
at some point
you hear your last name called out
and think *oh shit*
she too has a claim to it

and grant that intimacy
should it come
will never be the same again—

AGAIN

Who is
anxiously grinding the marble sculpture of our love to dust—

OUR LOVE

With great restraint
the wind preserves
the pebbles on your monuments
eventually they shift

first my sighs and the quickening
of my heart vibrate the little agates
then my invitation scatters them
thinking you skeletons have limits

THE INVITATION

Or you fall to the bottom
of the stairs and dogs
pick your bones clean

MOONSET

Helpless at their slow
suffering hanging from a cliff
Walter and Flossie see themselves

as separate but indivisible
from cancer and madness respectively
opposed to nursing homes as ever

their habitual road trip to Florida
has taken a vertiginous turn
in any event no one such as myself comes to see them

sweeping their last years with a searchlight
they are not making excuses
although they find themselves

on an untenable Hawaiian vacation
in a creative situation
like a cane field bent to survive

winds on the side of a mountain
because death has not proved enough
however it changes the whole brigade

if the leader could just look after
the spectators I didn't say *specters*
who've gotten stung down there

near their shaved sexes
in fact everyone please
go back to bed

it's impolite to see
transient bodies not above
begging

BEGGING

Whether or not it would explain our unwillingness
to score the severe damages
of a supreme being in our midst
it is a foggy morning tomorrow

TOMORROW

You let in a stranger
to your country unwillingly
that must have made
prompt Florence very angry
the blade at her throat
was that necessary?
granted she was unschooled and petty
but that was her hardwired
body about her a cloud of curls
how attractive she is captured
in rare chinchilla and gold lamé
photographed in the heyday of the Fontainebleau
we each know that in less than an hour
I will be at her graveside
in ways that seem shameful and degrading
abandoning her bones by droning
lines of Hebrew according to Law
where is the young man now
with his long hair and dark skin?

not worthy of the human one
who kneels here feebly

it is a lie that I can never recover

THAT I

Jane lolls at the beach
a shimmering hour goes by
impoverished bodies Walter and Flossie
swim leisurely as drops in the sea
they compare in significance
to the receptive spirit
they will enter later
when as monsters they return and with no one
noticing landfall
my nightmare of losing them is over

GONE

In my absence California grapes have tripled in size
spitballs I think but do not say
as usual it's as though we've just met
the man I idolize grows back

wavy blond hair and she need no longer dye hers
I have been burying as instructed
first their suffering then the human forms
finally their pains are no greater than their restraints

pontificating among the vines
with my little pail of blame
I come and go because I am a poet
who is endorsing these creations

CREATION

They survived their fires but barely
and then their bodies not at all
I'm thinking their deaths
take little effort
they work in a relaxed state they give
their attention with no excuses
but their illnesses nearly kill them
before they extinguish boundaries

BOUNDARIES

My images are fixed
for example the husband has on a hat and a topcoat
for another there is his wife in a swimsuit in her forties

with a little belly and an annoyed expression
something *fercockt* (Yiddish for *fucked*) with their morning
they retaliate with liver and onions for lunch

my memories vary but each is discrete
not like a movie but a book of poems
from another century a row of stone gargoyles—

someone's bothering their mouths with water

SAVING ME THE TROUBLE & THE TIME

I didn't hear the door open softly
I don't hear them freshen up in the bathtub
or notice their habit of walking their new dogs in the woods
I still think I'm alone

maybe she'll run the dishwater or complain about his television
I have no idea how hard they're working
to achieve humanity as much as their shadows allow
because it's hot they sweat on the backs of *their* necks also

MY HUMANITY

As a bride a woman is blindfolded
and tied to an ancient olive
this causes a tremendous gathering
a great need to rescue her future
children first of course
and then their cries

unless she can conjure a world
with lavender fields
without which I might never
have my little watery books
let's hope who knows what
fanciful thunderclap
can snap us out of it
like dead branches

or else don't read on

FRIGHTENING MOONLESSNESS

Once the family loops nature's warp
they wear (very transparent) masks

one's baldness and one's bare nape
give them away

they frighten me sometimes when I forget
I'm making love or reading poetry

apparently they want my attention
calling for water calling for air

the thoughts never enter my mind

AN OPTIMIST & A FANTASIST

Gorgeous and dangerous
like mountain fog

two little-known acts take place
to sugarcoat these ghosts

one is the optimistic setting
of flares so immortals

enjoy peak after luminous peak
therefore pleasure is blind

since the heavens are already lit
with souls wicking into glowing remains

(I hope they make it over the mountain
where citizens don't fight for breadcrumbs

like birds with numbers banded to their legs—
I could have said *branded*—)

the other act is a prayer
that god is not a vessel in distress

on a pillow of water upstream
finally going to drown

dreaming everybody's memory

MEMORY

Shouting *shayna maidel*
literally *beautiful unmarried female*
translation *pretty girl*

implied *open the goddamn door*
my savior breaks in on me
humping my boyfriend one afternoon

despite Bob Dylan protesting in stereo
behind a closed shade and door
Gary's hand is inside my pants

and I'm coming practically by breathing
Jesus whereupon she screams *what
in hell is going on?*

I swear on my mother's life in this poem
I will not let her despair
ruin a stranger's reputation

REPUTATION

We are ratted out
to Mr and Mrs Parents about

my foul self liquored up
whom their son delivers late

one Saturday night
as an abandoned newborn

to a wrought iron door
Your Honor does that now and again

come from the known world
to redress or esteem us

two teenagers working the loam
in the far east of Siberia

Pasternak's *back of beyond*
where the worst pupils sit in the class

my point being that shame
informs consciousness

WROUGHT IRON

The sun scorches the dusty leaves of New Jersey
probably all this takes place in July
because the lime trees are in bloom

regardless I become a lesbian from Kamchatka
bursting through the diamonds of my waxy fronds
as through burning glass

the sun brands the nuclear family
to his and her recliners in the den
until they're skeletons

COMES FROM THE SERVER THE SAME BANISHED WINES

They must be thinking their omnipotence
finally is vanquished
because my royals do not hesitate
in fact to save time
they grant entrance to their tower

this is what I am doing here
my neck hurts from licking my new darling's
smeared mascara and black bra
there is no moral to the story
I am too weak for the climb down her gold hair

NO ONE IS HOME WHERE I ONCE LIVED

When for Christ's sake
tonight? no! when then

will someone scarlet my black heart?

when I die
let the dead carry the red poppies

HAPPY BIRTHDAY

In her night-petaled black heaven

but for the missing teeth
one of the angrier angels is close to speaking
Hebrew ancestral words
I have failed to deliver

in the center of an otherwise
empty room
it is over for me I am on my knees
I sure as hell am

MY SEVERED HEAD

I touch my forefinger to thumb
and straighten the others for *bird*

for a shadow on a wall
of Faithful Heart's hospice

a far cry she whispers *from Florida*
I board her like a dog entirely

don't think I don't appreciate the gravity of my error
with my charge in diapers by a window

the Catalinas to the east weighted by snowflakes
I come to surrender

strange barking every night—strays? coyotes?

DEATH'S YELLOW HOSPITAL DRIP

Named for the martyred celebrant
caught marrying couples and beheaded
because the emperor believed
that erotic activity weakened his army
just as poor Valentine's farewell letter
to his jailer's daughter touched her lips

my lover meets my miserable soldier
on the last day of her life
says *thank you Flossie*

the broken yolk of narrative
I lived without her
sucks back into an egg

on the last day of life
there's a huge picture window of the sun
the horizon the mountain and the mind
chants about the sun the mountain the horizon
and the mind loop on a boom box
bought hurriedly from Target

warm compresses to mother's forehead
cool compresses to her lips
are you in pain are you in danger?
she seems to ask as I ask
I turn from one to the other
(her sun-flooded nightgown of gardenias)
(her smartly cut blond hair)

DEMYSTIFYING JANE

a mischief of mice
a mob of cattle
a charm of finches
a cast of hawks
a murder of crows

FEEDING THE QUIVERING NIGHTHAWK

As my patient's pupils whiten

they are like comets stopped
by a severe stare

it is like feeling the jet to death
the empty billeted corridor

it is like looking at a comet
and seeing the moving stairs to it

as welcoming
and bombed

SURRENDER

She enters my life with a great depression
undiagnosed it is metaphysical
before we come to carnage
we come to *rot in hell*
I am scared
I won't let her rest
in my dream I need to wake and feed her
with my leftovers
until my bones glisten in their majesty
of course she will be fine
the day in the desert is fine
it is the night-light
to the brightness where she is

MARRIAGE

The fare secures a shuttle journey from one stop
to the next across a grand canal or section

the journey is fissioned with children
shape-changing like clouds and rain

here and there clashes break out
among strangers who have paid too little

or too much expecting a longer ride
from fool's gold

not wanting the truth
as much as they want

to fill time like a locket
only to have it one day

ripped from their throats

LIKE A LOCKET

At one point I am on hold for the nurses' station

station—an outdoor arch from which night trains depart
with their little windows of puppet theater

fluorescent stations as small as nests
release passengers into tunnels of the western night

stationed far away
young men in goggles hurriedly become old men—

a nurse comes on the line—
nothing after midnight

a place? a person? poetry is filled with interpretations

A LITTLE MYTH

about me standing below a window
shouting *Valyntina! Valyntina*
until I'm joined by a couple of friends
who happen by
and others on their way to dinner
end up joining in the melody *Valyntina!*
who apparently is not home
I announce there is no Valyntina
there never was
a little perturbed but forgiving
the crowd dissolves into night mist
but one last voice
stays and tries again *Valyntina!*
it amounts to so little
yet poetry remains
on nearly every corner calling

She's got eyes of cornflower blue
eyelashed blond barely—

in the case of my wanting
Friday night done right

my love I almost wrote *lobster*

yes I want to be your lobster!
goodness there is an ice pick

between lover and lobster
who has the softest sweetest hands

I nearly said *plans*

what has happened
to (Freud's term) *the convulsive act*

of happiness—

flipped into a boiling pot?
drained and buttered?—

I thought better of myself then thought
cartilaginous claws nut-cracked to shard

you are the softest sweetest meat
I almost said *milk*

I may have

BLUE FIELD

—White & visionary before it is bloody

I imagine this is how it is black
water and sky together

rolling flooded by listening
as a fetus falling infolding

darkness drenched in rainwater

lying on yellow and green earth
dreaming purple and azure above

—then the cesarean

YELLOW FIELD

A jet taking off way
too fast
I tear from the uterine wall
I could have said *tear*
but if I am not born I am not going
to cry anymore

is this poisonous swimming hole our whole time together?
the whole time *I am like unto you* a fluid that bathes
I'm in need of being shorn

this is our bind
and my resistance
so we live apart the entire war

a heart hangs on a line and continues to beat
a beast hangs on a line and continues to bark

before long your children forget you both
are going
to be in need of being
buried

we are too weak
and yet by god we do it
we lock you each in the ground

but god is essentially freaked
I know because you get back
you get us back

into an abandoned home
a supernal zone
we master neither
the good nor the grandeur of

PURPLE FIELD

A flash of light ricochets off a skyscraper
onto a button on the svelte coat of a pedestrian
who finds herself in a car

then on a jet
next on a slow boat cruising for her missing
host and hostess too suddenly

the suburbs empty their syringes of anesthetic
finally screams from an emergency fill the hospital
I have gone with inquiries to *boost & ensure*

in your vernacular asked where to visit in the desert
my charge says she wishes to
gai kakhen afenyam—go shit in the ocean

the ocean responds roughly translated
zolst ligen in drerd—you should lie in the earth
loosely translated *drop dead*

so one makes one's peace with words
in a poem and with space in a dream
a family again

bullied bloodletted buried and bonded
as far as I can see
to the far reaches of the galaxy

the back of beyond
where nothing else fits
a green polka-dotted dress and a blue silk suit

on our beloveds as their images implore
they want to be restored
on the head of the pin of consciousness

CONSCIOUSNESS

A massive shadow of hubris
crashes through a universe of thorns

having no feathers but smooth skin
and wingflaps of nearly transparent

lugubrious membrane
there's lightning by firing of eyes

thunder by flapping of wings
cowboys leaving a trail of moonshine

fire at the heart of it
while the legend disappears

rumors persist of a big dead bird
nailed to a barn with a mighty span unfurled

and several men posed under it for scale

STATUES OF MOSS

In that old silver-mining town
as statues of moss in moonlight
we're still confused as to
whether dreams predict or record
such storms

forced from straw beds by vermin-men
to be extras with a "Spanish look"
rather than stand in shit and shovel
are taken to dance and act in a period romance
featuring the mists and babbling brooks of the Dolomites

also a wrestling scene with a shepherd
and a half-tamed wolf also Riefenstahl gives herself
the leading role of the gypsy girl
in cinched waists that would be all the rage

Goebbels complains about the money for *Tiefland*
calling it a *rat's nest*—a stab at poetry—
and orders the Spanish village of Roccabruna reconstructed
in Germany down to the scented oranges
which Jews can neither pick nor sniff

before they're sent back to the camps
and gassed by fear's sycophants
the auteur is making the final cut in Austria
saved from the bombing of the Babelsburg studios in Berlin
she's smoking a black-market cigarette

as I lay waste in my kitchen to any claim
for art as redemptive even if it can be made
beautiful and true and nothing more I grant you
it's an abuse of power of a minor order
compared with her gall to kiss the Führer

will it restore his humanity
if I return the shepherd to his hut
in this miserable world with his leg savaged?

and the story of a few Jews
under branches teeming with oranges

what good repeating their last breath?
and children of the Roma and Sinti
forced to run through the village behind the star
with tarot cards in their baggy pants
will you have them beg?

RAIN LILIES ARE GYPSIES TOO

Gypsies reappear after sleeping
as sprigs of pastel lilies
through the wrath of a thunderbird

~

PURPLE THISTLE

At a farm a temple or a stadium
apparently I am made to speak

my fellow mosquitoes and bees
suddenly quicken their applause

my funeral concludes briskly
I appreciate that something or someone stopped me

going on too long repeating scandals
why waste myself on them

having had the better of me forever
no the truth is in the body language

but the poor meat shriveled when cooked
what is amazing is that near

the ashes I've become two lovers
ply a fire higher and higher

like a good metaphor
for the changeling come to life

under a heap of last twigs
rattlesnake skin and cactus ribs

bright as bliss
if it would please

WRITTEN ON WATER

A little music from a missing flute
recites the events of the day

I could go to Los Angeles
that rowdy orchestra

or stay here like Hokusai the old man
mad about drawing

a little thistle or bellflower
a nervous wagtail in a snowfall

nothing gets written down
but someone must share it

while my skin ages and dries I empty
the dream bucket for my drinking friends

breathing is also easy
and cannot be thought

of reading and writing
the same may be said

ROMANTIC FIGURES

I dream my broken dolls home to Miami Beach
he's leaving for his second round of card-playing for the day

she's dressed him in a black polo shirt and matching slacks
stylish if funereal

about his winning hand and her helping hand
pink and melon oleanders

married fifty years
thinking they've been poisoned

I jump sweating into Mirabello Bay
quivering glass hotels on the water

QUIVERING GLASS

We pad about naked in the imaginary world
carrying liquid in our sieves

what time is it?
400 kisses o'clock

after twelve hours of sleep
Valyntina probably will be girlilicious

she's like making love in the afternoon with rose crystal
your mouth warms into pink sugar

granted the romantic figure for love
is not the simile it's the paradox

that she wakes herself snoring

WILD FIGS

Oleander olive mint
what have you

family money and power
nothing to lose

charcoal smoke from a taverna
and never need shoes

along these washed shores
spit into the sea and shout *Divorce!*

come home single and in love
with the enemy's young face at the window

the suicide bomber has boarded the bus
you must accompany her to the border

in the legend you die expected
but in this world there is only practice

STREET OF DREAMS

Whoever covered García Lorca
never identified his shallow grave

but finally one summer the mystery is told
it turns out he is likely very nearby

as a red poppy with a black heart
a field of him enchanted the site

until he was gathered
god is my witness thrown into a sack

and swung like a bag of cement into a trench
dug by some old soul seeking water in the countryside

huddling close by pomegranates or figs and possibly lemons
almonds and olives too are not uncommon

far enough from the villages to be out of sight
but you get there by car

since they would have needed headlights to shoot people at night
a firing squad of career policemen and volunteer executioners

half-afraid for their own lives murdered three others
and a poet for five hundred pesetas

one skank bragged
I gave that idiot a shot in the head

irony of ironies
while you attract fireflies gnats and other pests

nearby your own head

a hacked melon of red flesh
sweetens an empty marketplace

LET'S TAKE HOME ONE ROCK

After his defection
the famous footballer says

in broken English
that he wants his dictator

to keep going away forever
outside the embassy a car backfires

which one
not that one

in the confusion
he hears a childhood lullaby escape

a window of a raspberry apartment
building across the street

it is his one hope
of seeing his mother again

KNOWLEDGE

A stone another stone a hundred
thousand stones

watch BBC News tonight
along the coastline a man shot in the chest

shows the bullet hole calmly
like a dark boutonniere on his wedding day

an old woman in mourning clothes
brushes oregano twigs against a stone

without crushing the little buds
the mountain perfumes the mountain

LEAFLESS

At my age I'm approaching life
like a mosquito or a hummingbird

party to a great wind I remember
when I stayed up north with mother

on a visit to her sister they howled with laughter
a veritable monsoon cracking now

I'm lonely without them as they were without husbands
you cannot imagine what I dream her sister said at ninety

it is like entering enormous rooms and furnishing them
with mountains of fire and fiery fountains

I thought *I'll try*

SHEEP

So I squander the coin
and arrive to a dark room when I wake

beside a brilliant blond light
you let me know

you're not happy about it
your intuition nailed it

but you stand by
you let it happen

recut your diamond
becomes more valuable

do you believe in god asked the disciple
nobody answered

by not moving

GRANITE

In your granite bedroom
inside the wallet in your purse

I'm scavenging
your unfiltered thoughts

a page with your savings
in the lace of an unschooled scrawl

rather than burn on the moon
I hurl myself

against the cold door
because I pity the door

I can never revive the violin
locked without leaves in a tree

IN A TREE

Surrounded by seahorses on a windy day
in a seashell chariot the billionaire of foam

furious at the loss of the city
so named for accepting

a gift from Athena of an olive tree
because of its wood oil and fruit

rather than the salty watering hole he opened
by striking the ground with his trident

Poseidon tosses a monstrous flood
of coins impressed with the head of Athena

into the sea also lions and cowering bulls
beaten into gold surrender

Greeks plant the change in the jaws of the dead
who must pay to cross the underground river

Charon requires only one obol
while heroes come and go

penniless souls rove the banks restlessly
only Orpheus crosses because of his enchanting music

as a free spirit
you are perhaps familiar with the legend

toss a coin and you will return
but to find it under your tongue

the mind's eye must be beautiful and spacious
as a summer pasture

where a child beholds someone recently dead
in an owl

THE READER

She's buried her head
in a stiff white cloth hat iced

against the heat she's also flashing
a bikini winking *laugh* on her bottom

while she dreams charming idlers
the rest of the words dry on a line in the sun

where you keep reading
there's a cliff and when you fall off

you backstroke into the sea and when you are tired
come in for lamb chops and a nap

you must not refuse the meat
the Cretans are broiling all over the island

because at the end of the day
there are neither real lilies nor illusions

but as you read in your book you exist
as an almond floating through honey

THE REINCARNATED

Having barely escaped death today
furiously begetting nothing

after ten hours of writing
you cannot judge too harshly

the opportunistic forager
seizing warblers from feeders and nests

traveling downhill or in danger flying
a few seconds as a bronze gloss

you must be prudent if one races
slow-motion in front of your moving car

only to dart into brush
for the next thing you know

the lamp is lit and the eyeglasses await
the roadrunner as the reader

A ROSE PETAL

The Hopi believe the roadrunner
protects against evil

also kills fruit by a blow from its beak
or beats the neck of small mammals

against rock with ungodly speed
the adult will murder a scorpion or snake

on a terribly ardent morning
one stuns a dragonfly or hummingbird midair

or leaps from a dry riverbed
after low-flying unsuspecting white-throated swifts

if it's a good book
the reincarnated poet will not mind

being stabbed in the air
and clapped against granite

A YOUNG POET

Some prefer being a yellow rose petal
I learned when I traveled

a young poet saying a prayer
is a form of panic

for begging beauty
one can hardly blame the artist

sleeping like butter in the sun
taking no action for action

ABOUT THE AUTHOR

Jane Miller is the author of several collections of poetry and a book of essays on poetry, culture, and travel. A longtime resident of Tucson, she is with the faculty of the Creative Writing Program at the University of Arizona.

Poetry is vital to language and living. Since 1972, Copper Canyon Press has published extraordinary poetry from around the world to engage the imaginations and intellects of readers, writers, booksellers, librarians, teachers, students, and donors.

WE ARE GRATEFUL FOR THE MAJOR SUPPORT PROVIDED BY:

THE PAUL G. ALLEN
FAMILY FOUNDATION

Lannan

THE MAURER FAMILY
FOUNDATION

NATIONAL
ENDOWMENT
FOR THE ARTS

WASHINGTON STATE
ARTS COMMISSION

Anonymous

Arcadia Fund

John Branch

Diana and Jay Broze

Beroz Ferrell & The Point, LLC

Mimi Gardner Gates

Gull Industries, Inc.
on behalf of William and Ruth True

Mark Hamilton and Suzie Rapp

Carolyn and Robert Hedin

Steven Myron Holl

Rhoady and Jeanne Marie Lee

Maureen Lee and Mark Busto

Brice Marden

New Mexico Community Foundation

H. Stewart Parker

Penny and Jerry Peabody

Joseph C. Roberts

Cynthia Lovelace Sears and Frank Buxton

The Seattle Foundation

Dan Waggoner

Charles and Barbara Wright

The dedicated interns and faithful
volunteers of Copper Canyon Press

To learn more about underwriting Copper Canyon Press titles,
please call 360-385-4925 ext. 103

The Chinese character for poetry is made up of two parts: "word"
and "temple." It also serves as pressmark for
Copper Canyon Press.

The poems are set in Adobe Caslon.
Book design and composition by Phil Kovacevich.
Printed on archival-quality paper at McNaughton & Gunn, Inc.